Get Married i

Watch out, this one's go~~ing to blow your socks off.~~

It may be the closest thing you'll ever find to a marriage promise without a ring: The women you'll read about in this book used the STOP GETTING DUMPED! methods and married the men of their dreams in *three years or less*. (Try that one on for size!)

Follow the methods in this book and you could be happily married to your dream guy three years from today. It worked for us. It can work for you.

"I met my husband in a bar, and six months later he proposed to me on top of the Eiffel Tower. Now I'm married to the most amazing guy I've ever met."
—Lisa Daily

"I used many of the methods in this book, and I married a truly wonderful man who respects me as much as I respect myself—You don't have to settle."
—Kristin Mattlage

"These methods really work! My sweetie proposed after just a year and a half. Sometimes I'm amazed at how wonderful my life has turned out to be."
—Kimberly Ruth

STOP

All you need to know to make

GETTING

men fall madly in love with you

DUMPED!

LISA DAILY

Vermilion
LONDON

3 5 7 9 10 8 6 4 2

First published in 2002 by the Penguin Group

This edition first published in the United Kingdom
in 2003 by Vermilion,
an imprint of Ebury Press
Random House, 20 Vauxhall Bridge Road, London SW1V 2SA
www.randomhouse.co.uk

Random House Australia (Pty) Limited
20 Alfred Street, Milsons Point, Sydney,
New South Wales 2061, Australia

Random House New Zealand Limited
18 Poland Road, Glenfield, Auckland 10,
New Zealand

Random House South Africa (Pty) Limited
Endulini, 5a Jubilee Road,
Parktown 2193, South Africa

The Random House Group Limited Reg. No. 954009

Papers used by Vermilion are natural, recyclable products
made from wood grown in sustainable forests.

Printed and bound in the UK by
Bookmarque, Croydon, Surrey

A CIP catalogue record for this book is available from
the British Library

ISBN 0 09 188779 8

To the dream girls,
Mom, Kristin, Betsey, Alice, Kimberly, Margaret,
Tina and Lisa

And my dream guys,
Tom and Quinn

And to my Grandma Vernie,
who always wanted a writer in the family.

CONTENTS

CHAPTER 1

Get out of the dumpster, girl

First things first

You may wonder why I feel qualified to offer dating advice. After all, just who am I anyway? A shrink? A psychic? Your mother? None of the above. The fact is, I'm just a normal person like you. Now, I've certainly spent some time with a front row seat on the jerk parade. I was just lucky enough to have learned a few really important secrets about men and dating pretty early on.

Many of these methods came from the amazing, man-magnet women in my family, like my mom, and my darling, 70-something widowed aunt. My aunt is back in the dating pool after a long and happy marriage of almost fifty years. And while her friends are all complaining about the terrible man shortage, and duking it out for the scarce eligibles at bingo, my little auntie has gentlemen callers lined up down the driveway and around the block.

Some of the methods came from my little posse of girl-friends, as we bravely navigated the shark-infested waters of the dating pool. Using these simple secrets stopped me and the girls from making the mistakes our other friends kept making over and over. Of course, what we learned, we shared with each other. Together, we learned what works with men and what doesn't. More importantly, we learned how to STOP GETTING DUMPED!

Within just one year, four of my best girlfriends and I were all happily married. Two-and-a-half years earlier, we had all been single with few marriage prospects. The secrets you'll find in STOP GETTING DUMPED! worked for us. They can work for you.

Some men are fabulous
Some men are jerks

At this point, you may be feeling like men are the enemy. This is just not true. Many men are amazing and wonderful. Men will scrape the snow off your car windshield, let you nibble the rest of their chocolate turtle cheesecake when you didn't order your own, and put a strong hand on the small of your back when they pull you close on the dance floor. Their shirts smell great when you wear them as pajamas, and they'll get up in the middle of the night with no more protection than your pink flowered bathrobe and a table lamp to see what's lurking outside at two in the morning. Men can be wonderful, especially to the right girl.

Yes, it's true. Some men aren't so wonderful. They cheat. They don't call. They're indifferent. This book will help you avoid those types of men. Sure, the occasional bad guy may sneak in, but if you follow the methods in this book, your chances of meeting and keeping one of the good ones will increase dramatically.

Do these methods really work?

Absolutely. A few years ago, I met a guy named Tom in a bar. (Pretty much like thousands of people meet every day in bars—well, at least every weekend.) He was a catch, and I used about every secret in this book to snare him. Six months later, this sweetie proposed to me on top of the Eiffel Tower. A little more than a year later we married on a beautiful, romantic yacht in the San Diego Bay. My husband is successful, charming and handsome, and is still the most caring, romantic man I've ever encountered.

I'm not the only one with a fantastic story to tell. My closest girlfriends all used these secrets, and married the men of their dreams. One of them got engaged that same summer in a hot air balloon. Another, on the peak of a breathtaking mountain. Yet another, at a romantic bed and breakfast.

Respect for the dumped

I'll just cut to the chase here, because I know you're wondering. Yes, I've been dumped. I am, after all, human. The thing is, and I can say this with all honesty, it *only* happened on the rare (brain-dead) occasions I strayed from the STOP GETTING DUMPED! methods. Who knows why I ever drifted from the formula? Sometimes, when things are going along too easily, we tend to stop working as hard.

It only takes a little focus to meet and keep the man of your dreams. Stick to the STOP GETTING DUMPED! plan. It won't let you down.

And now, a word from the whiners

Some of the methods in this book might seem old-fashioned or anti-feminist. I can live with the criticism; these methods work. The bottom line is, you'll end up with the kind of man you've always wanted, and you'll enrich your own life (man or not) in the process. I come from a long line of strong, amazing women, feminists all, who taught me that feminism is all about *having the power to do whatever you want to do with your life*. For some women, that means being a Wall Street tycoon, or race car driver. For others, it's the June Cleaver option, the house with the white picket fence, an adoring husband and a couple of Elmo-addicted toddlers running around. Or, it could be a combination of all of the above, maybe the Wall Street–Elmo package. It's your prerogative to choose whatever life you want. And sorry, no matter what anyone says, wanting a husband and a family shouldn't get anybody kicked out of the sisterhood.

The core of feminism is supposed to be about giving women the choices to get what they want. If you want to marry a man that adores you, this book gives you a clear action plan to do just that.

Do the STOP GETTING DUMPED! methods encourage women to play games in order to snare some poor, unsuspecting, man? Absolutely not. Men think a certain way, and women think another way. This book simply offers a plan to work *with* the way a man's brain operates, instead of against it, which is what many women unknowingly do. This is about dating strategy. We use strategy in our finances. We use strategy in our careers. There's nothing wrong with using a little strategy in our personal lives.

The methods in this book work. I would never suggest lying or being dishonest; in fact, I recommend highly against dishonesty. If you follow these methods, you'll weed out the losers and users before you get some emotional attachment to them, and only spend your valuable time with the most promising candidates. The book simply provides a plan to put you in the best possible light, and allows the man in your life to see you for the desirable, amazing woman you are.

Are you really ready?

You may have bought this book in the midst of a breakup. I've certainly done this myself, wandering through the aisles of one of those mega-bookstores like love's refugee, clutching a 10-pack of Snickers, and searching for answers in the pages of a book.

If you're just getting over a breakup, make sure you give yourself time to heal before jumping back into dating. Sure, read the book, and begin to follow the steps. Chapters two and eleven can be especially healing after a breakup. Just hold off on the actual dating part a few weeks or months. It's usually a good idea not to start seeing anyone until the impulse has safely passed to vomit and/or cry every hour, or worse, throw your fork at some unsuspecting member of the offending sex.

Once the crisis period has passed, usually with the help of a few Nora Ephron movies and two tubes of frozen cookie dough eaten right out of the package, you may be ready to take the next careful steps.

A dream girl is born

Once you start feeling like yourself again, you're ready to start putting these methods to work. Keep these things focused in your mind:

1 You are in the process of becoming the kind of girl men dream of, and
2 You are empowering yourself to meet and keep the man of your dreams.

This book can show you the way. So turn up your stereo and blast out a few verses of "I Will Survive." Have a ceremonial torching of your ex's picture and try a brand-new attitude on for size. Starting today you're a dream girl.

You'll find me referring to you, and my group of girlfriends, as dream girls quite often in this book. Is it because I have a group of beauty queen friends with egos the size of Houston? No. Is it because I think you're a beauty queen with an ego the size of Houston? No again. (Actually, I do have one friend who is a beauty queen, but she's fantastically down-to-earth.) My guess is, we're all pretty much the same. We're women. We like shoes. We all have insecurities and fears, goals and dreams, bad days and good days. We all want to fall in love.

When I say dream girls, I'm not talking head-in-the-clouds, residing in Fantasyland kind of girls. I'm talking knockdown, drag-out, fabulous, smart, funny, sexy, fearless, I've-got-it-all-together-and-I-know-what-to-do-with-it women.

I'm talking kick-ass chicks here.

The reference to dream girls is aspirational. If you can believe it, you can be it. It's the best version of ourselves, the one we aspire to be. You know, the one that has a fantastic job, spends three days a week helping out at a soup kitchen, whose apartment is always spanking clean, and who always has the right shoes, no matter what the occasion. It's in you. And I just know you can pull it off.

Go out and be a dream girl.

Hope for the best, be prepared for the weird

If you keep getting dumped in relationships, if you're not being treated the way you want to be treated in your current relationship, if you are getting a lot of first dates (or a few first dates), but no second dates, STOP GETTING DUMPED! can work for you. Sure, it's radical. Absolutely some of the methods you'll find within these pages are strange. But, if you follow this advice, your days of being alone, rejected and unhappy with your relationship are numbered. I promise, it worked for me, and it can work for you. So read on, and STOP GETTING DUMPED!

CHAPTER 2

You'll never meet Prince Charming (or Prince William) unless you're ready to go to the ball

Peace, harmony and pedicures

Who knew something so important for you could be so much fun? Here's the first of the dream girl decrees: In order to feel really fabulous about yourself, confident and beautiful, and as comfortable in your own skin as you can, you must start caring for yourself. *Pampering* yourself. Remember, you're an amazing, wonderful girl. Don't just pamper yourself because this book says you should. Dream girls know they deserve it.

I'll just skim over the basics, because you already know what they are. Eat well. Drink lots of water. Exercise at least three times a week. Aside from being good for your body, exercise releases all those fabulous "happy" endorphins that give you that wonderful sense of well-being. (Kind of like shoe shopping, but not so expensive.) Also, exercise gives you that extra boost of energy you'll be needing when you get your rotation in full swing. (See chapter four.) Of course, you should check with your doctor before starting any exercise program.

Pampering yourself is crucial to your well-being, and to

the success of the STOP GETTING DUMPED! method. Even when your social schedule is jam-packed, you must always take time out to care for yourself. One of the original dream girls, Kimberly, is especially good about this one. Even though she puts in sixty-hour weeks as an advertising executive, and spends most every other free moment with her doting husband, she always manages to sneak away for her weekly manicure. She knows how important it is to her well-being.

Here's more. Get a fabulous dream girl haircut, and a trim at least every eight weeks. The dream girl haircut doesn't have anything to do with a particular style, it's whatever cut makes you feel like *Miss Thang,* and compels you to walk with a little swagger and spontaneously flip your hair like one of Charlie's Angels. You'll feel it right away. A part of you will halfway expect to look back and find trail of wolf-whistling construction workers and schoolboys following behind you, like you're some kind of female Pied Piper. When you get *that* feeling, you've found the right cut. A good stylist can be a godsend in guiding you toward the most flattering and stylish look for your face and hair type.

Regarding new hairstyles: Never cut bangs, or make a drastic permanent change for at least *one month after a breakup.* When you're smack-dab in the middle of an emotional train wreck, the last thing you need to deal with is a hair trauma. Wait a month or two. When your head has cleared, you'll be ready to make those appearance-altering decisions with clarity, and face the scissors with confidence.

Another sure pick-me-up is to try a new hair color. Go red, go blond, or go black. A new color can make you feel like a new person. My girlfriend Kristin was the queen of this particular move. Like the dream girls' own version of Linda Evangelista, she tried a dozen different hair colors just for kicks, and looked fabulous in every one of them. Be sure to get a professional color consultation when considering a change. An expert can help you choose the best shades for your coloring. Kristin is the only person I've ever met who could wear nearly any color and look smashing.

Make sure your clothes are flattering. Don't get caught up in trends unless they look utterly fabulous on you. Don't worry, if the hot trend isn't right for you, there will be another one coming along any minute. (Hey, kind of like men.)

Always dress as though you might meet "the guy" no matter where you're going. No, I'm not saying you should be sleeping, eating and pumping gas in a miniskirt and strappy sandals. Just be sure that no matter where you go, or what you're doing, you always look your best. Figure out the most flattering colors and styles for your coloring and body type, and wear them every day. If you're not sure, ask a couple of close girlfriends to be brutal with your duds, and pick their three favorite and most-hated of your outfits. If you keep hearing the same thing over and over (*Sure those pants are nice, if you're going for a truck-stop mechanic look...*) you can assume it's probably true. Look for patterns in their likes and dislikes. Does everybody love you in green? Wear more green! Keep hearing gray makes your complexion look like canned meat? Cut it out of your wardrobe, or at least don't wear it close to your face. Pay attention to what you're wearing on the days you receive the most compliments. Figure out what's causing the big stir, and whatever it is, color or style or both, wear more of it.

Refresh your lipstick throughout the day. Run a brush through your hair before you hit the street. Check your shoes for toilet paper before you leave a public restroom. (This is good advice for life, not just when you're looking to meet the man of your dreams.) Be prepared. That way, if you do end up meeting Mr. Right while you're out walking the dog, you won't have to strategically veil your face with your hand because you've got that little Fu Manchu thing growing on your chin.

Here's where it gets really good. The dream girls know it is terribly important to indulge in some little treat for yourself at least once a week. Get a body scrub, or a massage. Have your nails done or get the muck steamed out of your pores. Try the entire menu of girlie delights until you find what makes you feel the most beautiful and relaxed, and then do it over and over again like some kind of supermodel opiate. Aside from making your outside more beautiful, your soul will reap the benefits as well. There is nothing more important and soothing than caring for yourself as a standard of your life.

Now, I'm sure you're thinking—who does this book person think I am? Ivana Trump? I don't have the money to blow $85 on a facial every week!

I promise, I'm not insane. Not many of us have the money to do that. The fact is, you can indulge yourself with a myriad of girlie-girl treats for nothing more than hamburger money. Hey, I wouldn't insist you needed a facial every week without telling you how to get it, would I? Of course not!

Welcome to the bargain spa

So here's how it works: Start hanging out at your local beauty schools, or what the girls and I like to call "The Bargain Spa." You'll find them in the yellow pages, and almost every town and city has one. They're usually open during normal business hours for clients, and most are open on Saturday as well. Beauty schools are a haven for cheap treats. Here, you can get crème brûlée care for lime Jell-o prices. Students who need practice before their exams administer the treatments under the watchful eye of a licensed instructor. Of course, the key here is to only choose treatments that will wash off. Stay on the safe side—you don't want to accidentally end up with a 1978 perm, or only one eyebrow. It's best to go to your regular salon for anything that will permanently alter your appearance.

There are, however, a number of wonderful, pampering therapies to be had at the beauty school. And the best part is, they're dirt-cheap. Every city varies, but where I live, scalp treatments with a deep conditioner and 30-minute head massage go for as little as $5. Complete facials with a deep pore mask, can be had for $5. Pedicures are a steal as well, usually $3–$5. The best thing is that these students are working for a grade, so they'll give you extra time and attention you might not get at a busy city salon. Yes, girls, a $5 facial feels almost exactly the same as a $75 facial when you're in the dark with those little eye patches on, and that groovy new-age music playing in the background.

Once you start going on a regular basis, you'll get to know some of the students and find one or two who do a really fabulous job. I spent a year getting the most soothing and amazing facials every week from a fantastic, talented student named Sarah. I was her first regular client, and we became friends. She gave me all kinds of wonderful little insider tips, like what products to spend money on, and where to go cheap. (Good foundation and blush, cheap mascara.) Not only did my skin look ravishing, but she also gave me all sorts of free extras and experimented with various techniques and aromatherapies just for fun. I nearly cried when my husband and I moved away.

Another great tip for bargain basement pampering is your local massage school. They offer the same type of deals as the beauty schools, basically cheap massages by students who are working to get their credentials under a licensed instructor. And, as you might expect, a bad massage is quite a rarity. Hour-long massages by students typically cost anywhere from $5 to $20.

Now, this doesn't mean that you and your girlfriends shouldn't splurge once in a while and spend a day (or a week) at a *real* spa. There's something absolutely rapturous about hanging out with your girls, drinking green tea and padding from treatment to treatment in those fluffy white slippers.

If even $5 a week is too much of a stretch for your budget (hey, I've been there) you must still take time out every week to pamper yourself. Give yourself a drugstore facial, paint your own toes, and lie on the couch with a deep conditioner on your hair and a bag of frozen peas on your eyelids. Treat yourself well. If you don't lead the way, no one else will. And, after all, we dream girls *deserve* it.

CHAPTER 3

Never ask a man for a date

Your first move is to let him make the first move

Here, we enter the realm of the old-fashioned. This little secret is extremely important, though, no matter how outdated it may seem. *Never ask a man out on a date. Ever.*

Men need to be men, and bless them for that. The very same brain cells that make him need to be the instigator in the relationship are also the ones that cause him to give you his coat when it gets chilly outside, or kill the really big, nasty bug in your kitchen. These are good brain cells.

"Hold on," you might say. "What if my guy is just terribly shy and would never ask me out if I didn't make the first move?"

I know this may be a hard one to swallow, but here it is: The truth is, any man, no matter how shy, will muster the courage if he truly wants to ask you for a date. If he's shy, it might take him a while, but it will happen eventually. If it doesn't, he doesn't really want to date you. He might accept if you were to ask him out, out of kindness because he doesn't want to hurt your feelings, or even more likely, the possibility that you might be an easy mark for sex.

The truth is, if you ask a man out on a date, part of him

will believe you're desperate, and wonder what's wrong with you. After all, if you're so great, why isn't somebody else dating you? He may even go out with you a few times, but trust me, the relationship will be doomed. He will never truly value you, because of this simple fact: *He didn't have to work hard to get you.*

I hate to compare you to a rubber mouse, but . . .

Think of it this way. You have a cat, and he has a little rubber mouse toy. What's more fun for him? When you plop it down right in front of him, or when you tie it to a string, dangle it just out of paw's reach and run around the house like a lunatic while he chases it? Yes, that's right, Option B. Imagine in this little scenario, the man is the cat. You, my friend, would be the rubber mouse. (Sure, a bright, independent, sexy mouse, but still a mouse.) No matter what you've heard, it's a lot more fun for the man when you give good chase.

Men need to be the aggressors. As a woman, you get the wonderful job of either accepting or rejecting his advances. Men are not comfortable in that role, and will not take to it on a permanent basis. This is why you should *never* ask a man out on a date, and you should never instigate the relationship.

Now, I hate to admit it, but my girlfriends and I experimented with this one quite a bit. We approached men with varying levels of aggressiveness and creativity. We did the stare-at-the-guy-until-his-brain-melts routine. We jokingly claimed to be Dating Game chaperones, or members of an all-girl band. We told men we could own them for a dollar, and then proceeded to complete the purchase. All of these acts, and many more I'm too mortified to confess, garnered us a *lot* of attention. And frequently, we had half the men in the bar, concert or cruise boat clamoring for our attention. The end results, however, were ultimately the same. When we approached men, or met men halfway when they approached us, the guys were not nearly as active in pursuing us later, and the relationships were ultimately doomed.

In order for the methods in this book to work, you must allow the man to pursue you. As we all know, anything worth having is worth working for. Never deprive a man of the thrill of the chase.

Meet and greet

Once you start following the STOP GETTING DUMPED! methods, you should be meeting a lot more eligible men, and getting a lot more dates. Why? Aside from your compelling new demeanor, you'll be out and about, living your best life and having a fantastic time, factors that make it infinitely easier to meet men. It is important to remember that no matter where you meet a man, whether it is at the grocery store, a blind date, or even a game show, the fundamental rule is always the same. The man must pursue you.

Of course, there are a number of special circumstances that require a bit more guidance. If you are in a bar, or some other place, and see a man to whom you are attracted, you should smile and make eye contact with him just once or twice, but *do not approach him.* Try not to look at him more than once every fifteen minutes or so, even if he's utterly yummy. You don't have to stare a hole through his forehead for him to get the message. Your girlfriends can be immensely valuable in letting you know if he's checking you out without you having to look yourself. Relax and have a fantastic time, enjoying the company of your friends. If you're only there to scope out the joint, you might as well be wearing one of those big sandwich boards with DESPERATE painted on it in big red letters. If, after the first couple times you look up, you don't catch him looking back, stop right there. Do not send him a drink. Do not pursue him in any way. He must walk over to you, or you're out of business. Keep your feet cemented to the floor, or better yet, hit the dance floor with your girlfriends. If he is really interested in you, he'll come over and start talking.

The no-separation law

Another important rule applies when you meet a man out somewhere, especially in a bar. *The no-separation law.* This means, under no circumstances do you leave the bar/club/ bowling alley/disco concert with anyone but the girlfriends you came with. The dream girls always leave together. This isn't just important for safety, but for setting boundaries right away. If a man wants to spend a little more time with you, he'll just have to ask you for a date. This sends a clear message that you and your girlfriends are not on some sad man-hunting expedition, where you'll just ditch each other for anyone with a Y chromosome. Girl's Night Out is a sacred ritual.

This brings us to the next point. Never *offer* a man your phone number. If he wants it, he'll ask for it. I'm sure you're getting the hang of this by now, but here's something more. If a man *does* ask you for your number, don't ask him *when* he might be calling you, or *if* he's really going to call you. Don't give him your entire detailed-to-the-minute schedule for the next two weeks so he'll know exactly where, and how, to reach you, twenty-four hours a day. Assume that if you're following the STOP GETTING DUMPED! methods, and he's asking for your phone number, he'll call. After all, he did just make his way all the way across the bar, think of something compelling to say to a complete stranger, muster the courage to approach you and go way out on that scary, wobbly limb to ask for your phone number. All you had to do was stand there, be charming and try not to dribble your margarita on your cute little outfit. I'd say, you're off to a flying start. He's already put in some effort, and the scales are tipped in your favor because you didn't meet him halfway. He'll call. Just write your number down on the piece of paper he gives you. Don't hunt down a pen, or scrounge through your purse looking for a scrap of paper. This is important. Tell him you'll be happy to give him your telephone number, and then smile and wait patiently as he scours the bar for a writing utensil.

Freaks and freak accidents

Of course, there's always the odd exception to the rule. On the subject of those peculiar little men who ask for your phone number, and then *don't* call, the dream girls believe it's safe to assume after a few days that the poor dear was probably mowed down by a runaway tour bus, or had to suddenly leave the country due to some pressing national emergency. Don't take it personally, simply move on. If you're following the STOP GETTING DUMPED! methods, you'll have more than your fair share of men calling. The occasional drop off the radar screen is nothing to fret about.

CHAPTER 4

A pair and a spare: Using rotation until you find "The One"

Love's easy as 1,2,3

This was always one of my favorites of the STOP GETTING DUMPED! secrets, mostly because it's just so much darn fun.

Most women will date a man, or a few men, until they meet someone they might like, and then they immediately *stop* dating the other men. Now that they've given up their other guys, they focus all their energy and attention on the one guy they like.

Will he call? Will he ask me out on Saturday night? Should I hyphenate my name after we get married?

Pretty soon, the guy freaks out under the white-hot intensity of all your attention and dreams. And then, he bolts. And now, you are *not* dating the guy you really like, but you're also *not dating anybody else, either.* This is a mistake. And what you'll find below is how you correct it.

This is how it works: At all times you are not in an exclusive relationship, you date (rotate) three men. (The pair, and the spare.) In the event that you have a full rotation (dating three men), but someone new you would like to date asks you out, you simply drop your least-favorite suitor from the group, and add the new one.

Why would you do that? The reasons for dating three men at a time instead of one man at a time are simple:

First, rotation takes your mind off any one man

You're not worried about whether or not bachelor number one is going to ask you out on Saturday night, because if he doesn't, one of the other two will. Men can smell desperation a mile away, but the opposite is true as well. When they have competition, at some level, they sense it.

Dating three men keeps you from worrying about any one of them. If one isn't up to your standards, you always have another two. Plus, here's the kicker: They always want you a lot more when they're not sure how many players are in the game.

Second, dating three men at a time keeps your schedule pretty full

No kidding, right? This is good for several reasons. First, you get a lot of dates, so your grocery bill is bound to drop dramatically, leaving more cash on hand for essentials like herbal body wraps and building your stock portfolio. Second, you won't have to *play* hard to get, because you will *be* hard to get. And last, having so many men competing for your time is fabulous for your self-esteem. All the men will be wondering what you're doing with the time you're not available to go out with them. Besides giving you a more mysterious air, it really makes them crazy. Men are intensely competitive, and their attraction to you will increase tenfold if they sense another rooster in the chicken coop. As an added benefit, you'll never sit home waiting for the phone to ring. You'll be out on a date, or recuperating from one (maybe while napping on the couch with one of those little blue ice-masks) whether your phone rings or not. Meanwhile, the members of your rotation will each be trying to figure out how he can have you all for himself.

Third, you get to date three different guys at a time, without worrying if one of them is The One

This is really nice. Maybe bachelor number two loves to take you to see hip bands that number three has never even heard of. Maybe bachelor number three gives great foot massages, but doesn't share your interest in museums. No matter! The three of them combined will have no trouble satisfying all your dating needs. (Sort of a "Frankendate.") You are relaxed and happy because you always have a date on Friday nights (and probably Tuesday nights, too), and having all your needs met without feeling like you need to mold one of them into what you truly desire.

So now, you're dating, you're busy every weekend, you're having a ball. You're meeting nice people and you're still available for when the guy with all (or most) of the qualities you're looking for comes along. You just fold him into the rotation and give him a test drive.

Let's say you have a good rotation going but you're really starting to groove with bachelor number one. What do you do? Drop the other two? Are we dizzy on nail polish fumes? Absolutely not! Only after bachelor number one tells *you* that *he* wants to be exclusive (and he will), do you consider dropping the other two.

Don't say yes right away. Tell bachelor number one you'll give it some thought. After all, we don't want him to get too cocky, thinking you've just been waiting around for him to commit to you. While you're mulling it over, tell bachelors number two and three that they're great guys, but you think you need to see where this other relationship is going. They'll be crushed, of course, but they'll appreciate your straightforwardness and probably kick themselves for not being even more aggressive in their pursuit of you. As an added bonus, you'll probably be locked away in their minds as one of the good ones who got away.

Later, if bachelor number one doesn't prove to be as charming as he seems, you might even still have two good candidates for your next rotation. (Hey, there's nothing wrong with recycling.)

Next, tell bachelor number one that you've considered his proposal and that you can *try* it to see how it works out. Be sure to use the magic word, *try*. Why? This gives your guy the idea that this might be some type of probationary period, so instead of slacking off because he now has a committed girlfriend, he works even *harder* to please you than before. Marvelous, isn't it? Now, don't overdo this one, it's meant to be subtle. Don't tell him he's on probation, or tell him how long the period of "trying" will be. Just slip it in. Don't you worry, if you've been following the methods, he'll be on his toes already, and he'll pick right up on that magic word, *try*.

What to do, what to do

Finally, some quick answers to common questions about the rotation. First, what do you do if bachelor number two asks you for the commitment, and he's not the one? Politely decline, and tell him you're just not ready to go to that step with him right now. Second, what do you do about the guy you want to drop when you meet a man and you already have a full rotation? Kindly and gently tell him that he's a wonderful guy, but you just don't think it's working for you. Be as nice as you can. Remember, it sucks to be dumped. Especially by a dream girl.

You may wonder, why date three men, and not two or four? Three seems to be the magic number. Two doesn't keep you busy enough or offer enough variety, and four, well that feels less like dating and more like crowd control. An ambitious girl may be able to successfully rotate four men, but eventually we all have to dedicate a little time to important tasks like work, REM sleep and leg waxing.

One final note. Do not have sex while you are rotating men. You are a fun, desirable, spectacular girl. You are not a tramp.

CHAPTER 5

The 48 mandate

Good things come to those who call in advance

This is really critical. *Never accept a date unless the man has asked you out at least forty-eight hours in advance.* This means a man can call you no later than Wednesday for a Friday night date. The two-day rule applies to weekdays as well, although the dream girls and I always required at least a three-days-in-advance notice for Saturday night dates. The 48 mandate is important for several reasons:

First, it lets the man know right away that you are not sitting around waiting for him to call. You have a busy, active life, after all, and your time is in demand. This may initially come as a shock to him, but when he realizes you're not waiting around for him you'll be more appealing to him than ever. You may be concerned that a man will not ask you out again if you turn down a date. Amazingly, just the opposite is true! Maybe it's that competition thing again, who knows why it works.

Here's what happens: Instead of assuming you don't like him, he'll likely be more persistent, and ask you out next time with more notice. He'll probably spend a little time wondering where you are, and what you're doing without him. This stokes the competitive part of his brain a little, and then he starts thinking. If you're so popular, there must be something *really* fabulous about you. He will also get his first (and probably not last) taste of the fact that you are quite a busy girl, and that if he wants to spend time with you he'll have to plan ahead. Some men do this automatically; others need to be guided to more gentlemanly behavior.

Second, the 48 mandate keeps you from sitting around on a Friday night, waiting for a Mayday Man call. You know that if he hasn't called by Wednesday, you *must* make other plans for the Friday night, and stick to them. Make plans for dinner with any similarly situated girlfriends, book a pedicure, or go see a movie or an art exhibit with a co-worker. Whatever you do, make unbreakable plans with someone else. That way, when an uninitiated man calls you on Thursday afternoon, or worse Friday, for a Friday night date, you can sweetly and honestly tell him that you would have liked to go out with him, but, *gee*, you already have plans.

It is very important to make plans right away, once Wednesday evening rolls around and you find yourself dateless. Making plans with another person is a nice little extra safety net so that you won't be tempted to make any exceptions to the two-days-in-advance rule. Here's the extra bonus: Even when you don't have a date, you will still have a *life*! Just like magic! Date or not, you've accomplished two things. First, you're not waiting around your apartment on a Friday night in case your guy decides to call, watching some cheeseball television program, and wishing you had something to do. On the flip side, the man you're dating, having been turned down for too short notice, will spend more time thinking about you. Not such a bad deal, eh?

Now, obviously, this is more of an issue before you have a good rotation going. Once that happens, you'll have three men asking you out, all aware that your time books fast. Within no time, they'll create a lovely dynamic where two or three days won't be nearly enough notice to ensure a weekend date. All you'll have to do is keep track of what outfits you've already worn.

Pulling away brings them closer

Now we come to the every-third-weekend principle. It's a very good idea to go ahead and make plans with your girls, family and friends every third weekend or so, even when men have begun to ask you out every weekend. Go wild in Atlantic City with the girls, or hang out with your platonic guy friends at the beach. Aside from being loads of fun in itself, it serves a delightful purpose. It's that "having your own life" thing again. Besides, it keeps a man from becoming too comfortable with your availability to him, and, it's a good way to ensure that you don't blow off your friends just because you have a guy in your life. You'll find that by regularly pulling away from your guy, you'll actually cause him to want to spend even more time with you.

So, what about that cute little guy you meet on Friday who calls you first thing for a date on Saturday? Very sweet, but the 48 hour rule still applies. Trust me, he'll appreciate the date a lot more if he has to wait awhile. Now, the dream girls and I don't condone dishonesty, but this is one of those areas where it's okay to fudge a little. You must *always* tell a man who calls less than two days in advance that you have plans, just don't tell him they're with your cat, your bathrobe and a pint of Häagen-Dazs.

What about that one handsome, persuasive, charming man, your own personal romantic Achilles' heel, who calls you for a date on the same evening (or in the same hour)? No matter how fabulous he is, don't be tempted! If you accept, you're only teaching him that you're available when he doesn't have anything better to do. Boy, won't he get the shock of his life when he realizes that you are not like the other women he has dated. He will be intrigued to find out his charms no longer work on you, and you can take him or leave him.

Remember, you only want to date a guy who really *wants* to spend time with you, who *thinks* about spending time with you, and who *respects* you enough to treat you as though you have a life that is quite full with or without him. You are not a booty call or a last resort. You're a fabulous dream girl in high demand.

CHAPTER 6

Never call a man

Never EVER call a man

This one you may have heard before. There's a reason for that. It's because *you should never call a man.*

Let's take this one step further. Never call him first, and never return his calls. Why? Simple. In order for a man to be truly intrigued by you, he must do the pursuing. He must be the one thinking of you, and thinking of a good reason to call you. He will be the one giving chase. He'll be the one planning what to say, and wondering if *you* really want to talk to *him.* Best of all, every time you talk on the phone, it will be because *he wants to talk to you.* You'll never catch him at a bad time, or when he's in the middle of clipping his nose hairs or watching WrestleMania, so you'll always have his full attention and desire.

Now, obviously I'm talking about calls on a personal level here. I'm not saying you shouldn't call your male client if you're a salesperson, unless, of course, you're interested in him romantically. If you are interested in him, you should only contact him during business hours, and only on matters relating to business.

Now, you may be thinking of all kinds of reasons why it should be okay to call a man. What if he calls you first? What if he has lost your phone number? What if he tried to call during the three seconds when you were ordering pizza and he got a busy signal? What if, *gasp,* your phone is broken? Here's the answer: *Never call a man.* If he really wants to talk to you, he'll call back. If he loses your phone number, and he really wants to talk to you, he'll track you down. I know a man who went to the same club every single night for weeks in the hopes of seeing a girl whose number he had lost. Finally, he ran into a friend of her sister who hooked them up again. That romantic couple has been happily married for more than ten years. He also learned an entire foreign language just to communicate with her, but that's a different story. The point is this, if a man really wants to ask you out, he will find a way to do it.

You may think a man might assume you don't like him if you never call him back. That's incredibly logical, but it simply isn't true. Think of how difficult it can be to get a man you *don't* like to stop calling. You know, that geeky, persistent man who calls you night and day, brings you those tacky little convenience store roses wrapped in plastic, and asks you out for months even when you repeatedly tell him no?

Sure, it doesn't take all guys this long to get the hint. But something as ambiguous as not returning calls won't be seen as a rejection. After all, you haven't told him no. Men, if they notice at all, will see this as a challenge. My own darling husband asked me repeatedly during our dating phase to give him a call at work. I never did, and I must say, I believe it made him even more aggressive in his pursuit. After several years of marriage, he still calls me from his office every day to see how my day is going and tell me he's thinking about me. Will you talk less because you don't call him? Absolutely not. If anything, you'll speak more frequently. To men, it's all part of the wonderful challenge of the chase.

Bye-bye, love

Here's another point of enormous importance: Always end any phone conversation first. That way, you'll leave him craving more. This also applies to dates. *Always* be the one to end the date, and *never* see him more than a few times each week. He'll constantly feel like he wants and needs to spend more time with you. He'll be thinking about you, and wishing he could spend more time with you. How amazing is that? A man, sitting around his house, eating frozen cheesecake (we can dream), and thinking about you for a change! Before he knows what hit him, he'll have all kinds of pent-up romantic energy focused right at you. My husband used this particular energy to find unique ways of expressing his affection for me. Once, after a long day, he showed up at my door with his arms loaded with gifts: a bookstore treat, a bouquet of flowers and, here's the interesting one, peanut brittle.

It is the natural inclination of women to want to spend every waking moment with a new man. Unfortunately, this makes most men feel crowded. When *you* create a space between you and your man, it actually gives him a chance to miss you, and soon, he only wants to spend more time with you. Of course, you must continue to create that space on a regular basis, or else, that push-pull spell will be broken. Each time you pull away, the more closely he will follow. And that is a lovely thing.

The old drink-'n'-dial

Okay, I think we can all admit, we've done this at least once in our lives. You go out with friends, have a few (six) too many margaritas, and suddenly you find yourself back in your apartment at three in the morning with a little buzz and an overwhelming urge to chat.

So, you ring up your ex-boyfriend because you *really need* to talk to him *immediately* about crawfish seasoning or to tell him you *really* are doing just fine without him, *thank-you-very-much*. Or you call your current boyfriend to confess that you told your sister he might actually be *The One*. Next thing you know, you've left a slurred, garbly message bordering on insanity on the guy's answering machine, or worse, he picks up and you humiliate yourself live and in person.

When morning hits (or mid-afternoon, depending on how drunk you were) and the tequila has worn off, the realization hits you. And (gasp in horror) there's nothing you can do . . .

One of my closest girlfriends (whose identity I'll keep secret, or she'll kill me) was the queen of the drink 'n' dial. While the rest of us girls were rummaging through the kitchen looking for chips and salsa, she'd be talking away with some guy she hadn't seen since college. Thank goodness we lived on the east coast. She'd have caused some serious enemies calling in the wee hours from California.

If you're prone to such midnight phone compulsions, here's a simple solution: Before you go out, hide your cordless phone, or your phone cord, someplace weird like the freezer (unless your post-party favorite is ice cream, in which case you should probably go with a location such as the linen closet). The key here is to hide it somewhere strange enough that it's inconvenient to access, but close enough where you can get to it in case of trouble. That way, it's too much of a pain in the neck to call when the urge is strongest, and you can make it safely through the night until sanity returns.

CHAPTER 7

Smells like love

Scintillating cinnamon

Brace yourself, this one is a little wacky. This particular secret will seem really odd at first, but you'll be shocked at how effective it can be. According to some sources (including Dr. Alan Hirsch *and even aromatherapists*?!), men associate the scents of cinnamon and vanilla with love. Now, I'm no scientist, so I couldn't begin to tell you if it's some food/mom connection, or something deeper in their hardwiring—all I know is, it works.

About an hour before your date arrives to pick you up, pop some of those ready-made cinnamon rolls in the oven. If you're feeling really Martha, you can make homemade cinnamon bread, and impress the guy with your culinary prowess. If you don't have store-bought rolls on hand, and you're not handy in the kitchen, just throw some old bread in a pan, with a little milk and lots of cinnamon, sugar and vanilla. Put the mess in the oven and bake it at 325 degrees for a half hour to 45 minutes. When you take it out of the oven, it will be a horrific-looking blob of glop, and nothing you'd want to eat, but your house will smell undeniably fabulous. Whether you use the ready-made cinnamon rolls, or the cinnamon blob, your place will have a yummy, homey, cinnamon smell that men just can't get enough of. Yes, it's something akin to baking chocolate chip cookies when you're trying to sell your house, just formulated to zero in on guys. Your man probably won't have any idea why he feels so good and comfortable at your home, but he'll want to eat you up with a spoon.

There are candles and air-fresheners with the vanilla and cinnamon scents, and they're okay to use in a pinch. The other dream girls and I have found, however, that nothing works quite like the real thing.

My girlfriend and former roommate Betsey and I used this technique on a number of occasions with great success. It's easy, and it sure gives the men a better sense of direction when they're beating a path to your door.

If you like, you can take it a step further, and wear a subtle perfume with vanilla undertones, or a vanilla-scented lotion on your skin. Just be sure to put it on with a very light touch. The goal here is to make his heart pound, not his eyes water.

CHAPTER 8

Where dream girls meet their dream guys

Put him in the driver's seat

This one may seem a little odd, but like everything else in this book, it has a purpose. *Never pick up a man for your date. Never meet him at some "in-the-middle" location for your date.* If a man wants to see you, he must pick you up at your home or office. If safety is ever an issue, say it's a blind date or someone you met online, then by all means meet him in a public place. Just make sure it's on your home turf and completely convenient for you. Once again, the harder he has to work, and the more time he has to invest, the more valuable you will become to him. Sure, he may complain at first that it is easier for the two of you to meet halfway, but you can simply tell him that you prefer to be picked up at your door. Usually, this one is a no-brainer, because most traditional guys actually *prefer* to drive. My husband, after a year and a half of dating and several more years of marriage, has only been driven by me in a car twice. One of those was a trip to the Emergency Room.

The problem with meeting your date in the middle, or worse, driving yourself is this: You're just making things too easy for him. And, as you've probably realized by now, the easier he has it, the less he'll appreciate you. In a man's mind *more work = bigger payoff*. Besides, isn't his dream girl worth a little inconvenience? Absolutely.

Here's another little reason to let your gentleman drive. It's incredibly awkward for him to hold your door open if you are in the driver's seat. I don't know about you, but good manners have always been extremely important to me, plus I always needed that extra three seconds it takes the guy to go around to the driver's side to check the vanity mirror for any stray broccoli in the old pearly whites.

While we're on the subject, I'll clue you in on a little-known guy secret. A close male friend of mine says he always gives the girls he dates the "door test." Whenever he opens the car door for his date, he watches to see if she leans over to unlock the door on his side. If she unlocks the door, she passes. If she doesn't, well, let's just say, there's no re-test. Other guys have told me they look for the same thing, so girls, be sure to unlock!

CHAPTER 9

"Why buy the cow?"
Still true in today's meat market

No sex for the first month—really

Remember the old saying your mother or grandmother used to repeat, "Why buy the cow when you can get the milk for free?" Well, like it or not, in theory, it still holds true today. Sure the sexual revolution has loosened things up a bit, but as we all know, that old double standard still exists. So, you can either sit there, mentally debating with me about why it's unfair or wrong, or smile and do what works. I know you're a smart girl, and you'll make the right choice. After all, what's a little delayed gratification when we're talking about the man of your dreams? If you're following the STOP GETTING DUMPED! methods, you'll have the rest of your life to get wild in bed with this man. Whip out the fur-lined handcuffs and edible undies on your honeymoon, if you're so inclined. Now is not the time.

Try not to have a heart attack, it's really not that bad. Once you start dating exclusively, one more month really isn't that long to wait. Now, some dream girls, myself included, chose to wait at least two months before having sex. This is just an extra measure of certainty, to make sure the guy is really someone we want to be involved with on that level of intimacy. How long you wait is up to you, as long as you wait at least a month. After the one-month mark, it will be abundantly clear to your man that you do not take this sex thing lightly, and that someone would have to be pretty darn special before you'd consider jumping into bed with him.

The wife test is really a pop quiz

Why wait that long? Well, no matter what a man will tell you, they all secretly measure how quickly you sleep with them against that secret perception of acceptable wifely behavior they've got locked away in their brains. With most men, if you sleep with them too soon, you fail. Test over.

Another important key is *not* to tell the man about your self-imposed sex embargo. He might not take the time to get to know you, and woo you as he truly should, if he knows he just has to hang on until the finish line.

While we're on the subject, it's a wise idea to take things slowly in the first month on other fronts as well. Nothing but a kiss on the first date, and save the good stuff for later. The no-sex for the first month rule also applies to sex of the oral variety. Once your month of waiting is over, by all means, have at it. Just give yourself a little time before then.

This sex holdout isn't just for the man's benefit. It's for yours as well. Women tend to get more emotionally attached after having sex. The one-month waiting period gives you time to evaluate your man with a clear head, and without the romantic complications of sex.

Don't worry if you think the man will leave if you don't have sex with him. This simply isn't a factor. If he can't wait until you're ready, he certainly won't be hanging around long after the deed is done. By waiting, you are proving to your man that sex with you is something special, and he will have no choice but to believe you are worth the wait.

Plan B: Hairy legs

If delayed sexual gratification just isn't your strong suit, try this age-old trick for keeping things chaste. On your date, wear your rattiest, ugliest, elastic-challenged granny panties. You know, the ones you wear when you haven't done laundry in two-and-a-half weeks. There is no stronger motivation to keep your pants on than the possible exposure of ugly, anti-sexy panties. One of my girlfriends chose not to shave her legs if she thought there might be danger of things going too far. Another girlfriend wore clothes that were difficult to get in or out of. Do whatever you have to do, just make sure you keep it clean.

After you've been dating a few weeks, the question of "when" is bound to come up. Just tell your man that things are moving a little fast, and you're not quite ready yet. If this relationship truly has a possibility of going the distance, he'll wait. What's more, he'll probably enjoy it. Men love this particular challenge. There's nothing quite as delicious as that will-we-or-won't-we feeling in the pit of your stomach before the very first time.

Safety first

I would be remiss if I didn't stress the importance of safe sex. *Always, always, always* use a condom until you are both

1 in a long-term, monogamous relationship *and also*
2 have both been tested and are clean for STDs.

I'd love to tell you not to have unprotected sex at all until you are clean-tested *and* married, but if anything, I'm practical. We may be dream girls, but we're living in the real world.

Chapter 10

Get the check, lose the guy

Two to play, one to pay

Here's how the dream girls see it: If you're following the STOP GETTING DUMPED! methods, your man is asking you for the date, he is planning the date, and of course, as your host, he should always pay for the date.

First, it's traditional, and you're really a traditional girl at heart (which is why you want to meet a nice guy and fall in love in the first place). Second, a man who truly wants to spend time with you will be more than happy to pick up the check. Once again, he will value you more if he is doing most of the legwork for the two of you to be together. After all, he's investing his time, money and emotion in you, so he won't just hold you in greater esteem, he'll also continue to work even harder to keep you. Your man knows that nothing of value comes easily or cheaply. Your every action proves to this man that you are worth having. And he will be happy and challenged to pursue you because he believes it.

What's interesting is that most men tell me they really *prefer* to pay for dates. Men find it a little embarrassing and emasculating when the waiter presents the check, usually to him, and his date whips out the old MasterCard.

Rich girl, poor boy

Now, what happens, you might ask, if I make signifi-
cantly more money than my man? Well, that's fantastic for
you, really. The girls and I are very proud of you, especially
in this day of women making seventy-two cents to the dollar
for men.[1] But, of course, you're a dream girl, so success is to
be expected! The bottom line is still the same. Your guy
should pay for your dates.

Sock your money away and build yourself a nice big nest
egg. Sure, if he's cash-poor, he'll have to be a little more cre-
ative and take you to free concerts in the park or for picnics
at the botanical gardens, but once again, he'll appreciate you
more if he has to make an effort to be with you. A man who
truly wants to spend time with you will always find a way
(whether he has money or not) to do so.

Here's something interesting: The desire for men to pay
is deeply, deeply ingrained. My husband and I have been
married for a number of years and, of course, share our bank
accounts. When we go out, though, he still continues to make
the gentlemanly gesture of paying the check, even though it
is a joint account. My other married girlfriends report that
their husbands do the same thing. Obviously, good habits die
hard.

---

[1] Source: 1999 U.S. Bureau of the Census, Current Population Reports, p. 60, selected
issues U.S. Bureau of Labor Statistics.

CHAPTER 11

Don't count the days
Make the days count

Quick, get a life:
How to fake it till you make it

One reason men tend to break up with women is that the second a woman starts dating a man, she drops all her friends and interests, and relies solely on her boyfriend for happiness and a social life. This is, understandably, a lot of pressure for the man, most of whom are worried enough about things like car payments and receding hairlines without having to supply an entire existence for another person. I'm not sure why women do this. I've seen it happen dozens of times, and it is always perplexing.

Even without the man factor, it is important for every woman to have a life. Period. Not a "temporary" life of drive-thru roulette and night after night with the boob tube, waiting for your groom to arrive and your "real life" to begin. Create your own life. A complete, enjoyable life filled with dreams, career aspirations, friends, family, adventures and fun. You need to have a life, regardless of whether or not you have a man. Neither guys nor even chocolate are a suitable substitute for having a fabulous life!

So, how do you jump-start a life? Fake it till you make it. That means, visualizing yourself as a person with a busy, exciting life with plenty of opportunities to wear spectacular formal wear. (Or scuba wear, your choice.) Think of the exciting things you might do as that person, and then, put them into action. Plan a formal party. Get a better job. Meet exciting people.

You may have been waiting for your husband-to-be to show up before you start your "real life." This is a terrible plan! First of all, you will be missing out on all kinds of wonderful things that can only happen when you're not attached with two toddlers and a mortgage. Second, any truly fabulous man will want a woman who is her own person. Not a mannequin with a heartbeat.

What if your life sucks? Well that, fortunately, is all up to you. It's completely in your power to change. Think about what you love about your life and what you don't like. Then, and here's the tricky part, do *more* of what you love, and *less* of what you don't.

Hate your job? Dream about what you really want to do and start working toward it today. Even if you can only take one community college class a year, working toward your dream of becoming a veterinarian, it will make you feel happier to work toward something you love. My mom is an amazing example in this area. After many years of working at a career she was quite good in, but didn't love, she decided to start working toward a degree in early childhood development. Just a few months after she began taking classes toward her degree in that field, she was offered her dream job, as a director of a large child development center. She accepted the position and is still continuing her education today. Her career and life have taken a dramatic, positive turn for the better because she took the first step to do something she loved. Now we can't get her to leave the office!

Don't have any good friends? Join a newcomers group (even if you're an old-timer), buddy up with someone at work, reconnect with an old friend. Just make sure you keep people around you who support you, and help you feel good about yourself.

Bored with your life? Start planning adventures! Start with little weekend trips with your girlfriends, and go wild from there. Always wanted to go to Spain, but you were waiting for your honeymoon to go? Find a friend who loves adventure, or sign up with a tour group. Learn to hypnotize chickens, or skydive indoors. Stop waiting for someone else to show up before you enjoy your life.

Of course, the surefire way to having a better life is to always be open for adventure. The dream girls and I used to go on what we'd call "fun spontaneous girl" weekends. We'd take off to Atlantic City by train for a last-minute gambling adventure, head to Mardi Gras or Raleigh for a wild weekend of costume parties. Sometimes we'd save up and go all out for a weeklong vacation in some sun-drenched place like Cancun, sipping margaritas by the ocean, shopping like fanatics, and limbo-ing the night away with cute boys with thick accents and names we didn't recall by the time our hangovers wore off. There is great fun to be had when you're single. After you're married that chapter will, of course, close in your life. Enjoy every part of your life right now; otherwise, you may find yourself an old woman who's just been waiting around for the fun to start. The fun starts now.

Be open to opportunities. This is really important. If you think good things never happen to you, you'll be right. If you think your life is just one exciting adventure, you'll be right about that, too.

When I was at my first job, our agency won a national advertising award. Now, the award dinner was to be held in New York City, and being very far down on the totem pole, my name was not on the list to go. At the last minute, our CEO and VP had to back out, and the account person asked if I'd like to go in his place, since I'd worked on the account. Did it matter that the trip was only a few hours away, or that I'd be attending with mostly married senior partners in my firm? Not a bit. I grabbed my favorite little black dress and threw my cosmetic bag in a suitcase. A short time later, I was flying via private jet to New York, for a fantastic formal dinner. In a lucky break, one of my best girlfriends at the firm got the other open spot. Always ready for adventure, the two of us had the time of our lives on the company dime, riding around New York in a limo, drinking champagne and dancing at the Rainbow Room. On the way back to Virginia, we buzzed the Statue of Liberty in the private plane.

Just a couple years later, a man I'd been dating for just a few short months asked me to go to Europe with him for the summer. He was working in Italy for six months, and wanted me to join him. At first, I was hesitant; after all, I hadn't known him very long. I would have to quit my job and, yikes, find someone to care for my grouchy cat. But I kept thinking about how exciting it would be to spend the entire summer in Europe, and reasoned that if things didn't work out, I could simply come back. Well, as it turned out, things did work out. I had a wonderful adventure, I got to see some of the most incredible cities in the world, and I fell madly in love and got engaged in the most romantic city in the world, Paris. I am thankful every day not only that this opportunity presented itself to me, but also that I was brave enough to accept it. Of course, I am also thankful to Tom, my darling husband, who invited me in the first place.

Don't keep waiting for your "real" life to begin. If it hasn't begun yet, go ahead, start without it.

CHAPTER 12

Dream girls don't take any crap

You start today

People will only treat you as poorly as you allow yourself to be treated. Pardon my bluntness, but this is really one of the cornerstones of the STOP GETTING DUMPED! method. Think about it, and let it sink in for a few seconds. Make a pact with yourself, or better yet, with a close friend who is using the STOP GETTING DUMPED! secrets, too. From today forward, you don't settle for second (or third or eighth) best. That means the people you date. And the way you allow yourself to be treated.

No matter who you are, you deserve to be treated with dignity and love. You deserve to be romanced and cherished. If you follow your heart, and the secrets in this book, you will be. Set higher standards for yourself and stick with them. Think of it this way: You'll never get out of the dumpster if you keep hanging around with trash.

Here is the bottom line: Don't date anyone who makes you (or tries to make you) feel bad about yourself. Don't date anyone who abuses you, either physically or mentally. No one who loves you will belittle you, try to control you, or harm you physically. It's a fact. Even if they tell you otherwise, or claim to be sorry afterward.

My mom used to say, "Sorry means you won't do it again." Here's the thing about abusers, **they always do it again.** It's in their wiring. If you are in an abusive relationship, **get out now.** If you need help, call a hotline, or a shelter. There are good people who can help you get out any time of the day or night. Abuse is just not something you can be willing to tolerate.

If there's a Mrs., he's Mr. Wrong

Don't date anyone who is married. Even if it's the first time he's ever cheated (it's not) or he leaves his wife (which he won't) and marries you (which he won't), it will only be a matter of time before he leaves you for somebody else (which he will). Married men who cheat are notorious liars. They have to be.

If you date a married man, you'll never be number one. (His own wife isn't, why would you be?) You probably won't even be number two.

You'll spend holidays and nights alone with a quart of Chunky Monkey, waiting for the telephone to ring. You'll never have his full attention, because he'll always be thinking about the lie he's going to tell his wife when he gets home. Pretty soon, the best years of your life will have slipped by, while you're waiting for his wife to (insert pathetic excuse here), his kids to (more excuses), or his job to (more excuses). You'll have spent every New Year's Eve, Valentine's Day and family wedding alone, waiting around for a man who is clearly not waiting around for you.

No matter what he tells you, he doesn't love you. How do I know that? Because a man in love will do whatever he can to keep from hurting his partner. A married man fails on both counts. He's hurting his current partner by cheating on her. And he's hurting you by stealing your life and thinking only of himself. No matter *what* he tells you, he's still probably sleeping with his wife. That's what husbands, even lying, cheating, crappy husbands, do.

And, if all that isn't enough, consider this: Dating a married man means doing something that hurts another woman, his wife. If she's married to a sneaky cheater like him, she already has enough trouble to deal with without one of her own kind knifing her in the back. These types of men do enough terrible things all by themselves, we girls should stick together.

Stay with a cheater, cheat yourself

Don't date anyone who cheats on you. If it happens once, it will happen again. Why? If you stay with a man who has cheated on you, you've essentially taught him that he can sleep with somebody else and *you'll take him back.* Wow, that's pretty great news for him!

The first time he cheats on you, he has the most to lose because he doesn't know what your reaction will be. But once he's weathered the initial storm, he knows precisely how you'll react. By the time he's cheated on you twice, three times, thirty-eight times, he knows exactly what to expect. Lots of crying and screaming, followed by a few weeks or months of good behavior on his part. And then, he's on to his next aerobics instructor/co-worker/mall vendor. Repeat.

Even if you manage to get past the lies, the heartache and the ten pounds you'll put on with comfort food, a cloud will always hang over your relationship. You'll never truly feel cherished, or completely loved. And you deserve better than that, don't you? Why torture yourself with feelings of self-doubt and insecurity? Tell him to hit the road, lock yourself in your apartment with your closest girlfriends, a stack of sappy movies and a couple quarts of your favorite brand of frozen happiness. Move on, and find someone who gives you the love and respect you deserve.

During a particularly difficult time for my family, my jerk-radar was malfunctioning and I ended up dating the king of the cheaters. Having never dated anyone who had cheated on me before, I couldn't really believe it was happening. I felt awful, and isolated, and did not want this piece of garbage to leave me. When the smoke cleared in my family situation, I finally truly realized what I had actually known all along. This guy was not being true to me. I left him, got a little distance, and within days started feeling like my old self again. Looking back on it all, I don't know what I was thinking when I stayed with him. I do remember how *great* I felt when I *finally* kicked his sorry butt to the curb.

You have the power here. Let me say it again: People will only treat you as poorly (or as well) as you allow them to.

So, draw a line in the sand. As of today, your high standards are renewed.

Now that you're weeding out the losers, what will you do on Saturday night? Here's the answer: You'll only date people who treat you with respect and kindness and dignity. You'll only date people who are enthusiastic to be around you. I chose to date only men who brought me sweets and opened my car door as well, but that's optional, depending on your affinity for good manners and chocolate. From now on, you'll only date people who treat you as though you are a Christmas gift to the universe. This may narrow the field a little in the beginning, but once you get the hang of these methods, you'll have only the best men to choose from. And that's really what it's all about, isn't it?

The STOP GETTING DUMPED! method is not a magic wand. It will not turn a cheater or abuser into a prince. Consider him a lost cause and move on. The secrets you'll find here will help you to meet and maintain a relationship with the kind of man you truly want to be with. The other dream girls are behind you all the way.

CHAPTER 13

What to do if you're in a crappy relationship now

This is pretty simple

- ☛ Read the rest of this book, and diligently follow the STOP GETTING DUMPED! methods.
- ☛ If he doesn't shape up, dump him and start over with somebody new. Remember, you're not losing anything if he doesn't treat you like the spectacular, amazing girl you are.

If you're in a bad relationship, you'll have to be especially persistent in using these methods. If your man is treating you poorly, both of you have picked up some bad habits, which are sometimes hard to break. Use this book. He'll either treat you the way you deserve to be treated, or make way for someone who will.

CHAPTER 14

The dream girl—
a dream to be around

Above all, be yourself

This book gives you direction on a lot of things to do and say, but the intention is not to tell you how to be. You should always, of course, be your own thought-provoking, charming, funny, endearing self. The main goal here is to give you that extra something special that men find irresistible so they'll take the time to get to know the real you.

The great thing about the STOP GETTING DUMPED! secrets is that they give you the ability to have the man in your life eating right out of your hand, to pardon the expression. It is important to remember, though, that as enraptured with you as he will be, you shouldn't ever take advantage of his affection for you. Below you'll find a few things to avoid. A dream girl, above all, should be a dream to be around.

Don't

Don't be bitchy, or spiteful. Don't be cruel. Don't cheat. Don't lie. Don't be overly demanding. Don't be petty or mean. Don't hit. Don't be vindictive. Don't throw stuff. Don't treat him with any less kindness than you would hope for.

Snoops
(Or, Honey, I accidentally found this way in the back of your closet in the shoebox with the false bottom . . .)

Okay, let's get past the fact that in our greatest moments of weakness or weirdness most of us may have accidentally looked through our guy's medicine cabinet while he was otherwise occupied, or casually inventoried the gum wrappers in his coat pocket. Here's the bottom line: Snooping is bad news.

Aside from the fact that you should have no reason to mistrust your man if you are following the Stop Getting Dumped! methods, snooping will always get you in trouble. First, it's not very nice. Second, you could get caught in the act, which would be torturously embarrassing (and blow that whole confidence thing you've got going). Third, and this is a big one, if you do find something strange, even if it is innocent, it will eat you alive until you finally break down and ask your man how he came to be in possession of a condom signed by the Dallas Cowboy Cheerleaders, or a ticket stub to the Decorator Showcase. And then, ughhhh, you'll have to explain exactly how you know what you know. It won't be pretty. And, he'll probably have a perfectly logical explanation for whatever it is you found, and you will have humiliated and tortured yourself for nothing.

A side note: If you really feel you need to snoop to confirm what you already believe to be true (e.g., he's cheating on you), read and follow the rest of this chapter.

The green-eyed bitch

Yes, I'm talking about jealousy here. If you're following the STOP GETTING DUMPED! methods, there should be no need for it. Don't torture the poor guy and give him the third degree every time he leaves the room.

Usually, jealousy comes down to three things:

1 You've cheated on him, and you feel guilty about it, so you're tormenting him. You know better on this one. You shouldn't be cheating if you're in a monogamous relationship. If you are, you're more of a nightmare girl than a dream girl.

2 You're terribly insecure. This is no longer necessary. After all he's done to attract you in the first place, he'd have to be insane to think of cheating on you. Remember, you're not the same girl you were before. You have a full, exciting life, and confidence to the moon. Suck up those feelings of self-doubt, keep your mouth zipped, and do a reality check with a girlfriend. Insecurity of this magnitude is a relationship-killer.

3 Your female intuition is off the charts, and you really think he's cheating on you. Think about why you feel this way. Is there actual evidence of infidelity, or not? Phone numbers? Unexplained (or oddly explained) ab-

sences? Something creeping in the pit of your stomach? If not, see #2 above. If so, trust your instinct. Kick him to the curb. You don't need that kind of treatment. No one is worth that kind of heartache. He can be replaced.

A dream girl is always easy to be around. Just be yourself, and be nice.

CHAPTER 15

Never say it first: "I love you"

Nice girls finish last

I'm sure by now, you're starting to get the hang of the whole STOP GETTING DUMPED! method—letting your man pursue you while holding your own emotions in check in the early stages of dating.

When it comes to saying "I love you," once again, it is crucial to let the man take the lead in this important step in the relationship. Remember, men want to feel that they are leading the relationship. Most guys want to be with a woman that makes them feel like a man. Sure, any of us could manage to kill a spider in the kitchen when we're all alone, but stand squealing on top of a chair if there is a man with a rolled-up newspaper present. Are they any less afraid of spiders than we are? Probably not. Do they like that macho, protector-of-the-universe feeling when they've got the little spider corpse smashed all over the want ads? You bet.

If you try to control the relationship in an obvious way, like planning dates or telling him you love him before he says it, he'll back off. Exactly the opposite of what you want. If you simply control *your* actions in the relationship, using the methods I've described in this book, you'll have a lot more positive power in your relationship. Not only will your man be going down the path you want him to go down, he will strongly believe it's all his own idea. And don't we all like our own ideas the best?

Once again, if a man is the one deciding when to tell you he loves you, the timing will always be perfect for him. And, once again, you'll be in the easier position of accepting or rejecting his declaration of affection.

You may want to hear "I love you" a lot sooner than he says it, but trust me, he'll say it eventually. Some guys are a little shy about this one. I heard once somewhere that a man knows whether or not he is in love after just a few dates, while it takes a woman around a dozen dates before she starts feeling that way. I've asked a number of both men and women about this, and most felt that timeline was pretty much on the nose. So, keep this in mind when things seem like they're going well, and you start wondering when he's going to say those three little words. By the time you've started to feel it, he may have been feeling it for a while, and the big moment is likely imminent. Just be patient. You are, after all, the most secure, fabulous girl he's ever met, right? Of course he'll fall madly in love with you! Just be sure you let him say it first.

CHAPTER 16

Mum's the word on the "M" word

Insane, but true

Here's a pretty well-known fact. Most men are freaked out be the mere mention of the word "marriage." Even if they are happy and in love, for some reason, that one little word can send them running for cover. Here's the most important thing to remember: *Never say the word "marriage" to a man you are dating.*

This is quite a touchy subject. Who knows why that one little word puts fear in men's hearts and sends them frantically thumbing through their little black books (or Palm-Pilots) revisiting the ghosts of girlfriends past?

Most men I've talked to about this particular subject say it has something to do with the idea of feeling trapped or chained to one woman for the rest of their lives when there *might be* a supermodel brain surgeon getting a mocha latte on the very next block, just waiting to spend the rest of her life worshipping him. Maybe his business flight to Cleveland will crash land on a deserted island, and leave him stranded with 37 beautiful native girls wearing those uncomfortable little coconut bras. Sure, deep down, he knows the real you is a lot more fantastic than whatever he's afraid of missing, but to him, it's very real.

Here's a truly freaky thing about men. They are so fearful of this word that *any* mention, whether it's a intended or not, feels like a major hint to them. You tell him you plan to be married someday, he thinks you mean *to him, tomorrow.* If you tell him some fifth-grader from Spokane came in second in the National Spelling Bee because he misspelled the word "marriage," he'll think you're fishing for a ring. If you are chatting away about being a bridesmaid in your cousin Merrill's upcoming wedding, and how the dress is this horrifying fuchsia color that is going to make you look absolutely ill, and how you can't even imagine standing up through an hour-long ceremony in those hideous, and probably uncomfortable, sparkly shoes, he'll freak. Before you're even into the part about the rhinestone hair clips which are sure to make you look like a wanna-be Vegas showgirl, he'll get a glazed-over look in his eyes, and suddenly remember that today is the day he scheduled to get his bocce balls waxed. Why? He thinks you're pressuring him to get married.

You're probably thinking, Huh? Any woman on the planet would know you were talking about a purple organza nightmare, yet the man in your life will fear you are trying to find a way to drag him down the aisle. Sure, it doesn't make much sense, but here's your solution: Don't mention it. *Until you have said yes to his romantic proposal on bended knee, that terror-inducing word should never cross your lips.*

Another important point to remember is that men who want to propose get very wrapped up in the drama, romance and surprise of how to do it. (So, if you're talking about it all the time, it's not really going to be a surprise now, is it?) They relish the planning of what they hope will be the one of the biggest, most romantic moments of your lives. Left to his own devices, a man may propose in a myriad of incredible ways and places. My own husband plotted for weeks, and proposed to me on top of the Eiffel Tower. Other dream girls have equally romantic, tender stories to tell as well. One got engaged on the plateau of a breathtaking mountaintop. Another, after a spectacularly romantic proposal in a hot air balloon. Another of my girlfriends became engaged at a cozy bed and breakfast. Each of their men found a unique and special way to express his love, and ask his dream girl to become his wife.

Pressure doesn't always produce a diamond

There is an important lesson to be learned in all of this. Men, when pressured (even if it's only in their own minds) will retreat. Men left to their own feelings without pressure or expectation, will respond in ways so romantic we could never anticipate.

Here's something about men and marriage that is lesser known. As terrified as they are of hearing that little word, most men are actually quite comfortable with the idea of getting married, and may already be considering you as their prime candidate. This hardly seems to make sense, and yet, it's true. *Most men are reluctant to talk about marriage before they are ready to bring up the subject.* However, if they are the one to initiate the marriage talks, they're usually very comfortable with the act of getting married! Once a man goes through the action of planning and executing his big, romantic proposal, he can hardly wait to actually get married. This is a huge contrast to a man who gets engaged because his girlfriend tortures him to agree to go ring shopping until *he'd do almost about anything (including getting engaged when he has no intention of getting married) to get her to shut up about marriage for just one second* . . .

Just as a man who truly wants to ask you for a date will find a way to overcome everything from shyness to a foreign language, a man who wants to marry you will ask you himself. Don't think for one second he needs you to remind him of how much he loves you, or how much his mother thinks you make a nice couple, or how cute/smart/athletically gifted your children might be. If he wants to marry you, he's already thinking about those things. *If he's not already thinking about it, there's absolutely nothing you can or should do to push him in that direction.*

Last, look at it this way: Follow the STOP GETTING DUMPED! methods and you'll likely have a spontaneous, incredibly romantic engagement memory to share with your friends and grandchildren. Much, much better than a reluctant, foot-dragging engagement because you've been badgering the poor boy for months and he hesitantly caved after you and the jewelry store clerk had him cornered two-on-one.

CHAPTER 17

The dream girls' code of silence

So, we're nearing the end of the book here, but I still have a few words of wisdom to impart. First, the dream girls' code of silence: Don't tell your man (or any man) that you are following the **STOP GETTING DUMPED!** methods in this book. The poor guys are already a little suspicious sometimes, and probably won't read the book themselves. They're apt to be a little defensive if they believe you're reading some step-by-step manipulation manual, instead of understanding that **STOP GETTING DUMPED!** is really a book about how women can have better romantic relationships by fulfilling themselves, and by letting men be men.

Listed are a few no-nos for early date talk. Most of these things are far too personal to tell a man before he has confessed that he's in love with you. It's always best to wait at least several (four to six at the absolute minimum) months before spilling your life story. Always remember, your date is not your therapist. If you need therapy, by all means, see a qualified counselor. The key here is to be your most fun and charming self, to put your best strappy shoe forward, to be open to and interested in what your date is all about.

The key to good dating talk is in being a good listener, and in allowing the lighter, flirtier, more positive side of your personality to be revealed. Here are some subjects to avoid in the first months of dating:

- ☞ Don't talk about psychotic ex-boyfriends or horrendous ex-husbands. He may ask, but he doesn't really want to know. Change the subject.
- ☞ Don't talk about your horrible childhood, your yarn phobia or the fact that you can really see yourself as one of those old ladies with fifty-nine cats.
- ☞ Don't talk about STOP GETTING DUMPED! methods.
- ☞ Don't talk about how you really want to find a husband, or how your biological clock is nothing more than just a skin-coated time bomb.
- ☞ Don't talk about being used by men. Don't express a negative attitude about men. If you feel that way, you shouldn't be dating now. You should be either in therapy, or working through it on a marathon shopping binge with the girls. (Depending on the depth of your negativity, a temporary slump can usually be cured with four or five fabulous pairs of shoes, especially if they're on sale. More serious problems require actual professional assistance.)
- ☞ If you're *in* therapy, don't mention it.
- ☞ Don't ask to meet his family and/or friends. When he's ready for you to meet his frat buddies or Great Aunt Thelma, as with everything else, he'll let you know.
- ☞ Instead of spending the whole night doing the hard sell of yourself, *ask him* questions (not about mar-

riage or kids, of course). Make sure you spend more than half the date listening rather than talking. Find out if this guy is really someone you'd like to get to know better. Or not.

☛ If he asks you personal questions, questions about things you'd rather not talk about, or questions about subjects you should avoid, don't lie, but smile, and change the subject quickly. You'll avoid those trouble areas, and be more mysterious, to boot.

☛ If you have kids, don't spend the whole night talking about them. Even though they're really amazing. For a first date, names and ages only. After that, you can add five minutes of kid talk each date. (Five minutes on the second date, ten minutes on the third date, etc.)

☛ Avoid any subjects that are controversial, such as politics and abortion, for the first few months. You'll find out soon enough where each other stands, and the last thing you want is to get into a verbal smackdown over linguine and clams. Get to know each other first. The goal is to find out what you have in common. Start small.

Well, that's pretty much it. You are a unique and spectacular girl, *a dream girl.* Not only that, you are now armed and ready to meet and keep the man you've always dreamed of.

Best wishes for an amazing life, and great love. You're ready!

ASK LISA!

Dream girl strategies for real-world dating dilemmas
Q & A

As a dating columnist, I've received lots of letters asking for advice on specific problems. Following, you'll find answers to the most common questions.

For further dating information not covered in this book, the author can be reached at:

Ask Lisa!
Stop Getting Dumped!
P.O. Box 19442
Minneapolis, MN 55419

www.stopgettingdumped.com

love@stopgettingdumped.com

Dear Lisa,

I was with this guy a while ago. We lost touch and he got together with my friend, without knowing we were friends. They broke up—she lied to him and cheated on him. She is still in love with him, but this guy and I are still attracted to each other. Would it be a bad thing for me to get back together with him?

Okay, I know this isn't what you want to hear, but here it is: This girl is your friend, which means this guy is off-limits, no matter what she did to him. Even if he's great, he's not the one for you if he's dated your friend. This is a rule you should live by.

One more thing, you might want to rethink this particular friend. First, she dated your ex-boyfriend (bad friend move), plus she lies and cheats. Not exactly a stunning resume. If her other qualities aren't stellar, I'd consider giving her the boot.

You deserve to be respected and treated well by friends and boyfriends both. Don't settle for anything less.

Best wishes,
Lisa

Dear Lisa,

What if my boyfriend doesn't orgasm all the time when we are making love. Can I still get pregnant?

Yes. Yes. Yes.

Use a condom every single time you have sex.

It only takes one sperm to get you pregnant, and frankly, they start sneaking out long before the orgasm. Pregnancy aside, there are all kinds of horrible diseases and problems out there in the world right now, orgasm or not. AIDS, herpes, and about a thousand others come to mind.

Please use a condom EVERY TIME YOU HAVE SEX. If, for some reason, you won't do that, at the very least, use some other method of birth control. Talk to your doctor, or go to a Planned Parenthood clinic. They can help you figure out what will work best for you. But, if you ask me, condoms are best.

Best wishes,
Lisa

Dear Lisa,

She's 24, I'm 51. We've been living together 18 months. I think the world of her, treat her like a queen, she gets anything she wants. She's totally spoiled. I've been away for months now working abroad, with only short breaks home. During that time she's been having an affair with a (married) guy around her own age. When I found out, she decided to move in with him in a place that she rented for them. I went back abroad to work with a broken heart.

Her thing with the guy lasted two weeks, she threw him out when she discovered he was still sleeping with his wife. But now she's so embarrassed about the whole thing, she wants to leave town, to get away from him, all her friends, and me. I told her I still love her and will forgive her, but she won't even consider coming back to me. We're still on opposite sides of the Atlantic, so how should I proceed?

It sounds like you're a pretty sweet guy, and I'm truly sorry this has happened to you.

I know this is not what you want to hear, but here it is: She may love you, she may have made a mistake, and you may be willing to forgive her, but she is not capable of being in a relationship with you, or for that matter, anyone right now. How do I know this? First, you treat her like a princess (which you should, good for you) and she cheats on you. But who does she cheat on you with? A married man. A man who is clearly not available. She sabotages a solid relationship for one that has little, if any, chance of being successful. Think about what she's told you about her past relationships—has she been hurt a lot? cheated on? lied to? betrayed? My guess is that she seeks out this scenario over and over in her relationships, which only reinforces what she already believes: She is not worthy of being loved and men will always leave her. If she happens to end up in a loving relationship (like yours) she will sabotage it herself (and once again, prove what she already believes to be true). Eventually, she may recognize the pattern in herself, and take steps to change. Or, she may not. Unfortunately, only she can do that, and it may not happen for years.

My advice to you, as difficult as it may be, is to find a way to work through this breakup. You deserve to be with someone you can trust, who loves and cherishes you, and treats you with respect.

I am completely thrilled to hear you say you treat the woman in your life like a queen, and I hope it is something you continue in your next relationship. I am concerned though, that you would be so willing to take someone back who cheated on you. Here's why: If you stay with someone who cheats on you, you are teaching her without a doubt that she can sleep with someone else, and you will stick around. The next time, she'll know exactly what your penalty is for cheating (nothing) , and she will do it over and over and over again.

You deserve better than that. I promise, if you keep looking, you'll find it. A lot of fantastic women are looking for a sweet guy like you.

Best wishes,
Lisa

Dear Lisa,
   How do you tell if your ex still has feelings for you?

It kind of depends on the guy. Most men will start courtship behavior again, calling frequently, asking you out on dates (even platonic dates, just to test the waters), doing things for you that only a boyfriend would do (like washing your car, or giving you his jacket when it gets cold). Some body language experts say that a man will frequently pull up his socks when he is attracted to you.

I can't tell from your letter whether you're hoping he has feelings, or wondering if he has feelings, so I'll just tell you this: Trust your gut on this one; you probably already know the answer.

Best wishes,
Lisa

Dear Lisa,

Say you're a guy going out with a girl at a restaurant, and you have money but your girlfriend wants to pay for the dinner.

Who pays for the meal? Her or me?

It's very sweet that she has offered to pay, but most men will say thanks and pay for dinner anyway. You know she appreciates you, because she's made the offer, but you're a sweet guy, so you get the check. You'll always win big points if you do the gentlemanly thing.

Best wishes,
Lisa

Dear Lisa,

    What is the makeup of a perfect man?

    A: The perfect man is the man that is perfect for you. Generally speaking, he'll be kind, considerate in bed and life, self-sufficient, drug-free, employed, romantic, sane and attractive. The rest of the list depends on you. My perfect guy opens my car door, knows how to hold me on the dance floor, and kills (or liberates) any big ugly bugs that manage to sneak into the house. Your list is up to you.

    Don't settle. You'll find him.

Best wishes,
Lisa

Dear Lisa,

How do I forgive my boyfriend for cheating on me with his ex-girlfriend, whom I literally hate? He says he is sorry and I really believe he is, but it is so hard. I want to believe he will never do it again. Please give me some advice.

I know you don't want to hear this right now, but I'm going to give it to you straight.

I know how badly you want to believe he'll never do it again, but chances are he will. If you stay with a man that has cheated on you, you are teaching him (without a doubt) that he can sleep with someone else, and you will not leave. Wow, that's like the cheater's jackpot! The first time he cheated on you, he had the greatest risk, because he was taking the chance of sleeping with someone else *without* knowing how you'd react. Now he knows for sure. You'll cry, you'll be angry, you'll be mistrustful, and you'll stay. Which sadly gives him the green light to do this to you over and over again, which he undoubtedly will. Tell him to hit the bricks, you deserve (and will find) much better than this cheater.

As for the ex-girlfriend, of course you hate her. She slept with your boyfriend. I assume she knew about you, which is why you're not so fond of her. Women who sleep with some-one else's man don't deserve to be called women. Whether she knew about you two or not, let your anger toward her go. If she did know, she's just mean and doesn't deserve an-other minute of your time or energy. If she didn't know, you two are in the same boat. She's probably been jerked around by this guy as much as you have. Focus that anger on your cheating boyfriend, where it belongs, and then show him the door.

You deserve to be cherished, and treated with love and respect. Don't settle for anything less.

Best wishes,
Lisa

Dear Lisa,

I'm 25 and having a major attraction to my professor. I would normally be against situations like this, as I try to stay in my own age range. (He's 40.) He is extremely intelligent, funny and handsome. We email about 3–4 times a day and talk in his office all of the time. We are always laughing hysterically. I think this is beyond the realm of normalcy. (Is it?) There is acknowledged sexual tension. What should I do?

It's not the age difference that makes this such a bad deal, it's the fact that he is your professor, and you are his student. First, and foremost, you hit the nail right on the head when you said, "I would normally be against situations like this"— you're a smart girl, and you're right. You should steer as clear of this relationship as possible. This is not a good situation for you to get into, for several reasons. First, it is most undoubtedly against your school's policy for students and professors to date, so simply having a relationship with this man is jeopardizing his career.

But, enough about his problems. Let's talk about this from your side. A relationship like this will always be unbalanced, because he already has the power. You are his student, and that imbalance of power dynamic is bound to carry over into other areas as well. This relationship will be as lopsided as a boss-employee, or psychologist-patient relationship would be. And I hate to break it to you, but you will be the one who gets the short end of the stick. The other concern is, as great as he is, you have to be a little wary of a man who will so easily engage in something that is clearly taboo. I understand completely that you have a chemistry with this man, and I know how powerful that can be. I just believe if you really think it through you'll agree—you should pass on this guy.

Stay strong,
Lisa

Dear Lisa,

What is up with men? What exactly do they want? How do you let a man know that he is all you think about? That you would run to the ends of the earth for him?

Here's your answer. Men want a challenge. Don't tell a man he is all you think about—that's the first step to pushing him out the door. Get a grip here, sweetie. Spend more time with your friends, more time on doing things that make you feel confident and good (other than him) and less time focused on your guy. *Much* less time focusing on your guy. If you pull away a little, he'll come running. If you keep pursuing him, he'll bolt. If you want this man to be yours, you've got to keep him guessing a little. Confessing you'd go to the ends of the earth for him will only set you up for heartbreak. Not a good plan!

Best wishes,
Lisa

Dear Lisa,

OK, I need the works. How do I walk, talk, look, smile, laugh and do everything else sexy? I am 200 lbs, but I don't look fat. I want to look attractive. I have four days of vacation from school and I hope I can get myself together by then.

Sexy is on the inside, honey, not the outside. There are plenty of fabulous, sexy, full-figured women. Look at Emme, from E!, or Camryn Manheim. They've got it inside and out, up and down.

It's all about the attitude. If you think you're sexy and irresistible, you will be. Focus on your best features and use them to your advantage. If you want to feel good about yourself, do something to care for yourself every day. Give yourself a pedicure, or a facial. Go to an exercise class. Go through your closet and throw out everything that isn't flattering. Sit down and make a list of all your good qualities, and the things about you that are unique. Do something for yourself every single day. If you care for yourself, it will show in your attitude and in your self-esteem. A confident, together woman is sexy. Which means, if you care for yourself, *you'll* be sexy. You'll walk sexy, talk sexy, and be sexy. It's all inside, girl.

Go!
Lisa

Dear Lisa,

I made the mistake of breaking up with my boyfriend of a year a couple of months ago. We see each other once or twice a week for sex. I do it because I hope each time that I'll be able to stay the night and we can cuddle again.

He is in a "player" stage right now. Two months ago we were about to move in together, and now, I'm starting to feel like he just wants me for sex. Is there any way I can get him back? If not, how do I get over him? I cry myself to sleep almost every night hoping and wishing. HELP!

Wow, this is a hard situation. You've asked two questions: How do I get over him, and can I get him back?

It sounds like your boyfriend is doing either one of two things: Either he's still angry with you about breaking up with him, and he's acting out some kind of revenge; or during your breakup he decided he likes the single life (being a player), but also the familiarity of you at the same time. Lucky him, he's been able to have both. Either way, it's a no-win situation for you. You must get out of this bad pattern of giving him sex in return for affection. I know it sucks, but this is not going to bring him back. He won't just realize in the middle of the night that he can't live without you. He WILL, however, know that because of your feelings for him, you're essentially available for a booty call whenever he decides to dial the phone.

Here's what you do. First, you'll have to get over him (easier said than done, but not impossible). Then, when you're feeling like yourself again, and have broken out of this terribly painful pattern, if you still want him, you might see about getting him back. Getting through the hurt you're feeling now and taking the first steps to getting over him are your priority for now. Otherwise, you'll go on being miserable for months or years, with no resolution. Take action now.

Give yourself one weekend to sit around in your pajamas, crying and eating ice cream and watching chick flicks. Then, put your get-over-him plan into action. I guarantee you'll feel infinitely better in just a month.

First, don't call him. Don't talk to him. Don't e-mail him. Don't see him. Don't meet him. Turn your answering machine on, and screen your calls. It's clear you really have feelings for this guy and you're feeling pretty fragile right now. Take him out of the equation so you can begin to get a little stronger. I'm not saying you should never talk to him again, but I'd avoid him altogether for at least a month. That will give you a little time to build up your defenses. Don't mention to your ex-boyfriend that you won't be talking to him anymore, just cut off all communication. Believe it or not, this will help down the road, if you *do* decide you want him back.

Next, think of the relationship as over. I know this is tough, especially right now, but truly, it is. Grieve for what was, but consider it dead and gone.

Third, get out of the house with your girlfriends. Make plans for Friday and Saturday nights. Go someplace you can dance (that's one of the great things about being girls—we can dance in a group and nobody cares). The music and the physical activity will make you feel tons better. Start small, with a girls' night out, no men allowed. Maybe begin planning a trip with just your girlfriends, a weekend getaway, or an actual vacation (maybe a spa vacation). This will give you not only something to look forward to, but some much needed bonding time as well. Nothing works better to get a girl through a nasty breakup than a little chick bonding. Short on funds? Tell the girls you need a slumber party. Make daiquiris in the blender and give each other pedicures. Make sure you make plans every Friday and Saturday night for at least the next month. When you start feeling like you need a rest, you're on your way.

Fourth, exercise four or five times a week for the first week, then three times a week after that. Go to Body Pump, or run, or just dance like a lunatic in your living room. Get your heart rate going. Aside from making your body look good, exercise makes you feel good and boosts your mood. It's also a great releaser for stress.

Last, it sounds like you really crave the physical affection. Go get a massage. If you call your local massage school, you can get cheap massages by students (supervised by instructors)—generally not more than $15–$20. Do it once a week until you're through this black period (usually not more than a month). Another possibility, go get a makeover at one of the nicer department store makeup counters.

Best wishes,
Lisa

Dear Lisa,

How do I mend a broken heart? I had a relationship with this guy for three and a half years. We broke up last April, because of me being so protective and nagging. I always control him, I always bring up the past. I don't trust him. I love him so much that I made him my life. Then I found out that he had a girlfriend already. When I asked him about it, he told me that he doesn't love the girl. I tried winning him back, but he told me that he's not yet ready to be my boyfriend. He's afraid that the things that happened before will happen again.

I tried going back to him and he told me that he's not yet ready to commit. He calls me every day, but he calls the other girl too. He says he loves me and I'm wondering if he's doing the same with her. Do I have to let him go?

Why do you want to be with someone who won't commit to you, who cheats on you, and who leaves you in such a general state of misery?

You sound in your letter as though you have some control (insecurity) issues. Have you always been insecure? Or is it just with this guy? If this is an ongoing problem, you should think about talking to a professional therapist. If it's just happening with your current boyfriend, you need to think of *why* it's happening. Probably, there's a part of you that knows this guy is setting you up for heartbreak. The insecurity is (rightly) telling you this guy is a danger to your well-being.

I know this will be hard to hear, but you need to start over with a clean slate. He's already made it clear to you with both actions and words that he's not ready to be with you. And you deserve better than to be strung along.

Break up with him. And give yourself a break from dating until you can get your head straight again. Spend time with your friends. Take care of yourself—give yourself a little treat. Focus on school, or your work, and do something fun every single day. Don't let this guy back into your heart. He doesn't deserve it. You should be with someone who loves you and treats you like a princess. Don't settle for anything less.

Best wishes,
Lisa

Dear Lisa,

I hate to sound sexist, but it's been my experience that there are many men who claim they've been "burned" in a past divorce with material things and so they prey on the more dependent woman. Because, if a woman does not own anything much, or especially any property that she got from a man in any prior divorce, the commitment-phobic man rationalizes she is "safe" and won't "rip him off" for something.

I hate to sound cynical but I've also found that these types of guys come on really strong and then later down the road realize that they really didn't want a financially strapped woman after all, so they dump them.

This can have disastrous consequences for the trusting woman who believed the man's promises for security and caring assistance. The woman usually gets booted out on the street.

How can I protect myself from these types and recognize them in advance?

Here's how you avoid "Men who prey on dependent women"—Don't be a dependent woman! Support yourself. Begin to secure your own future. Work at something you love. Have your own interests. Do things with your friends. Don't drop everything for any guy who decides to call you at the last minute. Hold the men you date to a high standard. Refuse to date anyone who doesn't treat you like the whole, wonderful, valuable person you are. Be your own person. You'll find men WANT to take care of a woman who they know can take care of herself.

Good luck,
Lisa

Dear Lisa,
  How do I propose to a girl?

My husband proposed to me on top of the Eiffel Tower in Paris —very romantic. The same year, several of my closest friends got engaged as well: one on a mountaintop in Virginia, another at a romantic bed and breakfast, another in a hot air balloon.

There are a million possibilities. Maybe the place you first met, or a place she has wanted to go since she was a child. Give her a great story to tell the grandkids.

Use your imagination! You're asking this question, so you must be an incredibly romantic guy. You'll think of something spectacular.

Good luck!!
Lisa

Dear Lisa,

I have been with my boyfriend for a long time and gradually found that he had a serious mental problem, a psychological problem. I have spent a long time trying to help him to recover but it didn't work. I am very tired. What should I do? Should I give him up and begin my new life?

Yes. It seems like you're ready to move on. Sadly, there's not a lot you can do to help him with his problem, he has to do that for himself. You've done all you can, and it didn't work. Obviously, you're a good person, and the idea of leaving him is difficult for you. Just remember, you are deserving of your own happiness as well. Move on, and begin your new life. You will eventually find a romantic partner that gives you at least as much as he takes from you. You deserve nothing less.

Good luck,
Lisa

Dear Lisa,

What is up with men? What exactly do they want? How do you let a man know that he is all you think about? That you would run to the end of the earth for him?

Here's your answer. Most men want a challenge. Don't tell a man he is all you think about, that's the first step to crowding him out the door. Get a grip here, sweetie. Spend more time with your friends, more time on doing things that make you feel confident and good (other than him) and less time focused on your guy. Much less time focusing on your guy. If you pull away a little, he'll come running. If you keep chasing him, he'll run the other way. If you want this man to be yours, you've got to do your own thing and keep him guessing a little. Confessing you'd go to the ends of the earth for him isn't exactly going to keep him on his toes, but it will get him sprinting out the door.

Kisses,
Lisa

Dear Lisa,

What do you think about Internet dating, and meeting people online? Does it ever work?

I think Internet dating is a fantastic way to meet people. Online dating definitely gives you a lot more options than you would have if you stuck to your own school or your own backyard.

A few key points to remember:

First, never give out personal information right away. (Not exactly a newsflash, but still, REALLY important.) This person may seem like Prince Fabulous, but it's difficult to tell from e-mail. For all you know, your e-mail pal could be romancing you from her cell in upstate New York.

Don't post a fake photo or lie. If you end up meeting your online date in person, she is definitely going to notice that you are not the Abercrombie and Fitch model in your photo. (Really. Even if you suck in your stomach through the whole date.) Be honest and meet somebody who likes you for you. There are millions of people dating online right now — at least one of them is bound to like you exactly the way you are. (Two, if your mother's online.)

Last, be safe. If you're going to meet, do it in a public place, and if you can, bring a few friends along. If your online dream guy is chatting you up from his jail cell, you don't want to end up in the trunk of his pal Louie's '78 Thunderbird.

Safety first,
Lisa

Dear Lisa,

I've been with my boyfriend for three years. I moved back with my parents temporarily because we were fighting a lot. While I was home, he was seeing this girl he works with. I was really upset about everything even though she said she never had sex with him. She assured me that she would never talk to him, but lately she has been calling him again. I don't want to put up with this, what can I do to get this girl to stop calling my boyfriend?

What can you do to get her to stop calling your boyfriend? Get a new boyfriend.

I never understood why many women, smart women, when faced with a cheater will blame the girl he's cheating with. Maybe it's some short-circuit in our hardwiring. Like, *Gee*, my man is banging somebody else and that is... hm... the fault of the complete stranger who doesn't know me? Or my darling who swears he loves me but has problems keeping his pants zipped? It's her fault! That slut!

He is the one with the commitment to you, not her. She's just someone who happens to sleep with other peoples' boyfriends. Frankly, her type are like roaches. You can squish one if you catch her, but there are always more. And unfortunately, your boyfriend is the roach motel.

Also, just where is your guy while all of these calling/not calling negotiations are going on? If anyone's going to get this chick off the phone, it's got to be him. If he were serious about his relationship with you, he'd quit being such a two-timer and end it. It's my guess he likes the attention. And maybe, he likes having his girlfriend crazy all the time about what he's doing, and frankly, who he's doing.

What do you do? My advice is to dump him. Tell him to pack his CDs, ratty t-shirts and his condom collection and hit the street. You were already fighting all the time, he cheated on you, and now he's adding insult to tramps by disrespecting your feelings and keeping in contact with her. You deserve to be with someone you can trust, and frankly, once someone cheats on you, it's pretty hard (and not too smart) to trust him again. Why make yourself crazy? There's someone out there who will love, adore and respect you, who will not screw around. Find that guy, he's a lot more fun. And check yourself out of the roach motel.

Kisses,
Lisa

Dear Lisa,

My son's father and I have never been married. We'd only been dating for a

month when I found out I was pregnant. We moved in together and stayed together until our son was 4 months old. Whenever he and his girlfriend break up he comes to me. He's done this several times and I always end up getting hurt. This time though, we've actually been going on dates and talking on the phone daily, and he's been seeing his son more regularly. Do you think he is just playing me?

I've always been in love with him and know there is something between us. I want to believe that he's really changing and wants to work things out and get back together, but I keep thinking that he's just going to end up hurting me again. Any suggestions?

I know this is going to be difficult, but my suggestion is that you listen to what your intuition is telling you. In case you have any doubts, let me play it back to you:

"He's done this several times and I always end up getting hurt."

"I keep thinking that he is just going to end up hurting me again."

Sure, occasionally people change. But mostly, they stay the same. I think you already know what you don't want to believe – that a relationship with this man is a bad idea. There's a reason why this guy keeps coming back to you.

Unfortunately, I don't think it's love. I think it's because you let him. Set your standards a lot higher girl, you deserve it. And so does your baby.

Best,
Lisa

Dear Lisa,

I have a dating dilemma. I have been utilizing an online dating service and have met many nice guys. These men will take me out the first time and say that they don't want to date anyone else or take their name off the site after meeting me. How can I let them know that they aren't the only one I am dating? I feel I need to be honest with them, but also don't want to reveal my personal business to them either.

First, let me commend you for not jumping into an exclusive relationship with someone you've dated only once. Good for you!

Second, remember that if your guy friends choose to stop dating other women the second they meet you, well, that's really fabulous. However, you are under no obligation to do the same. Don't feel you must confess your dating habits to someone you barely know. Your other dates are your own private business. You can maintain your honesty by telling the truth if they ask you if you're seeing other people and by being perfectly honest (either way) if they ask for exclusivity. If your answer is yes, then ditch the other guys, if it's no, or not yet, simply say you're just not quite ready to take things to that level yet.

Kisses,
Lisa

Dear Lisa,

I just met a great guy. He's intelligent, sexy and classy.

We had lunch last Sunday, it ended up lasting for about seven hours. During our lunch he showed me some modeling pictures that he had taken earlier. He also showed me two photocopied images of himself naked, because he said he knew I'd be comfortable with them. He said that they were pictures that were taken by his girlfriend even though the pictures looked professionally taken. Later that night as we were making out he pulled out his unit which looked to be about 10 inches long and very thick. How can I tell if he's had a penal implant?

I am afraid that all he wants from me is sex. I noticed a condom in his pocket on our date. How do I keep from getting sexual with men on the first date? This has already cost me men in the past.

I am tired of the pump and dump lifestyle so please help me stop acting like a slut. I am a good person, but for some reason when I am attracted to a guy, I always get frisky too soon. When should I get intimate with a guy? Is it possible to build a lasting relationship with someone that I sleep with by the 2nd date?

Thanks

Girl, I don't even know where to start with this one.

You begin by saying he's sexy and classy, and just two sentences later he's showing you naked pictures of himself (during lunch, no less.) I'm guessing you're basing your sexy/classy observation on something other than that creepy move.

Is it possible to build a lasting relationship with someone you sleep with on the second date? Sure, but it's not very likely. As unfair as it may be, most guys don't want to be with a woman they perceive to be easy. True, it's an unfair double standard, (after all, he's doing it too,) but it is a reality. The other drawback to sleeping with a man too soon is that we women tend to get emotionally attached to someone we're having sex with much more quickly. Give yourself a little time to get to know and evaluate a guy to see if he's actually someone you're interested in being with, before post-sex bliss makes your judgment hazy.

Clearly, you're not happy with what you call the "pump and dump." So, how can you keep from hopping into bed right away? Well, for starters, try to wait at least a month before you start sleeping with a guy. If you're having trouble controlling your desire, you'll need a fallback plan. Here it is: Wear your ugliest, rattiest, granny panties on your date. (See chapter 9.) If you need extra reinforcement, don't shave your legs. Or your armpits. There is no greater motivator for a woman to keep her clothes on than prickly legs and the possible exposure of revolting underwear.

To answer your concern that your classy guy has had himself surgically enhanced, we consulted an expert in the field of penile surgery. Dr. Gary Alter, a Beverly Hills plastic surgeon and Assistant Clinical Professor of Plastic Surgery at UCLA, says that a surgically enlarged penis may look somewhat irregular (like being 10 inches long, for instance) and may feel lumpy or firm in certain areas if the girth has been enlarged. Depending on the technique used, the enhanced gentleman may have a scar in the pubic area or at the end of the penis.

If you're truly looking for a lasting relationship, set your standards a little higher and remember that you are a fabulous, unique, amazing woman deserving of love. Which means you don't call yourself a slut. You don't sleep with men you barely know. And you don't accept a second date from someone who whips out naked photos on the first date.

Best wishes,
Lisa

Dear Lisa,

I was seeing this guy for about three months, things were going fairly well but we didn't have a lot of time for each other. I told him that I wanted more of his time and I felt that he was just around for sex. He, of course, said it wasn't just sex and we were both just really busy.

So we stopped seeing each other for a couple of weeks. Then I wanted to see him again so I told him I would be more accepting of the fact that he is busy and that I would try to make more time for him in my schedule. He said okay, but still we didn't see each other very often and when we did, we had sex. Finally I told him I needed to know what was going on and what he really wanted. I told him if he didn't know that I couldn't wait around. He told me not to wait then and that he felt backed in. I always let him go out with his friends whenever he wanted, without being upset about it. I asked him if he had been seeing anyone else or if he was interested in seeing someone else and he said no, and he is trustworthy.

So I asked him why he feels like he can't be committed because it seems like for the last three months he has been. Even though we decided to stop seeing each other I feel like he is still interested but for some reason is holding back. I haven't been with or dated this guy in about two months but I can't get him out of my mind, I really like him. What should I do, or what can I do to get him interested again.

Thanks.

Wow, this is a tough one. I don't think you're going to like what I have to say, but I'm going to give it to you straight. Sometimes when someone tells us something we don't really want to hear, we kind of gloss it over in our minds and hear only what we want to hear. Clearly you have strong feelings for this guy, but I think you might not be hearing what he's telling you.

He has not been committed to you. He is squeezing you into his busy schedule for sex. If he had strong feelings for you, he would make time for you in his life in between the frat parties and daytime soaps. He is holding back, because he doesn't want a relationship with you (other than the one he currently has – a sexual relationship with no commitment.) It's probably true that he's not interested in anyone else romantically, but he's not interested in you that way either. I think he's been trying to tell you that in every way he knows how.

That said, why in the world are you so devoted to a guy who is clearly not devoted to you? With very little encouragement, you have volunteered to be his girlfriend-on-call, and rearrange your schedule so he can continue his lack of commitment to you. Why would you want to be with someone who clearly has no interest in being with you? Sweetie, you deserve better than that! There's a big difference between compromising for love, and in BEING compromised. I'm afraid you're being compromised.

Make a pact with yourself to stop today. You're not a doormat, you're an amazing, unique woman and you deserve to be loved and treated with respect.

Realize that you are worth more, much more, and don't settle for any man who doesn't treat you as such. A man who is in love will make time to be with you, and will treat you well. In the future, I'd let your dates pursue you. That way, you'll know what their interests are before you commit your heart.

Kisses,
Lisa

Dear Lisa:

I met this amazing guy two months ago. We're from two different cities so we have been emailing back and forth to each other. He came across as so sincere, sensitive and sweet. I have never met a guy like him.

So about three weeks ago, he decided to drive up to see me. Seeing this guy this person was just too much. We were so connected and it was out of this world. We both fell in love with each other. After he'd gone back, he emailed me like usual, and I did the same. And then, something strange happened, he

left a beautiful, loving voicemail for me over three weeks ago and I left another voicemail for him two days later and that was it! I have never heard back from him.

Please, did he just take an easy way out? Why didn't he even call or email to "break up" with me?

Let me start out by saying that there are just some guys in life that appear to drop off the face of the earth a few days after you have a fabulously amazing time together. Do they develop amnesia? Get hit by runaway tour buses? Get snatched by aliens or multi-level marketers for medical experiments and routine brainwashing? Who knows? Don't beat yourself up about it – it just happens.

In your case, however, something seems a little strange. Something in my gut is telling me there's something a little fishy with this guy – maybe a girlfriend. It's possible that the sudden stop in communication has happened because he 1) suddenly felt guilty, or 2) he was discovered and he's busy getting himself out of the doghouse with chick number one.

Either way, I'd put him out of your mind until he contacts you and it's clear his amnesia has been miraculously cured and that he's not otherwise involved. As for why he didn't call to break up with you – the reason is simple. Any breakup is bound to be an uncomfortable situation, and many men will try to avoid what they perceive will be a long, drawn-out, talk-it-to-death tearfest.

Kisses,
Lisa

HERE WE ARE, DREAM GIRLS.

We've reached the end. Thanks for reading this little book. I hope you've enjoyed it, and will put it to good use. Always remember how wonderful you are, and don't settle for anyone who doesn't treat you like the amazing dream girl you are.

If you need more information on anything in this book, visit our website at www.stopgettingdumped.com.

To receive the STOP GETTING DUMPED! dating tips news-letter, send an e-mail to love@stopgettingdumped.com with SUBSCRIBE in the subject line.

If you have questions, comments or stories about the book, or the STOP GETTING DUMPED! methods, the author can be reached at:

love@stopgettingdumped.com

Ask Lisa!
Stop Getting Dumped!
PO Box 19442
Minneapolis, MN 55419